I0483512

THE ESSENTIAL ENCAUSTICS

*Sixty-three Tips
So-you-don't-have-to-
spend-time-researching-
rather-than-painting-
Booklet*

Little Books of Wisdom.

Copyright © 2010 by Bela R. Fidel.

ISBN: Booklet   9780-9825484-2-4

All rights reserved

Table of Contents

Foreword

Why I Wrote this Booklet

When I first started to work with encaustics I was not familiar with the available resources and did not know anyone else who was working with this medium on a regular basis.

I had many questions and little knowledge and expertise. Most of all, I did not know where to go to find the answers. Everything took a long time which frustrated me very much. Instead of spending more time painting I was researching, trying to learn tidbits of details here and there, answers to bigger questions that arose with my experimentation. I had ideas I could not bring to fruition for lack of information. Along the way, I was trying not to pester the very few people with whom I had become acquainted, who were practicing encaustic painting and had more experience than I.

Ten years later, I had enough answers to compile this booklet and make it easier for others who are as enamored with this medium as I am.

With practice, you will come to realize that there is no end to the opportunities offered by working with encaustics. Every possibility will entail learning something new, experimenting, taking risks. I am sure the information contained in this Booklet will smoothly float you to increasing levels of expertise. You will spend more time painting and much less time seeking answers to basic but important questions.

You will find some sections in this booklet that provide seemingly contradictory information, such as the use of pure beeswax, microcrystalline and medium. This is because I provide information from other artists, as well as my own experience.

As you progress in your own practice, you will find methods and materials that work for you. Keep an open mind and be open to experimentation. The information in this booklet aims at making you comfortable with a variety of ways of using encaustics.

Introduction

Encaustic painting was practiced by Greek artists from the 2nd Century BC to the 4th Century AD, subsequently spreading to Rome. Initially, about the 5th Century B.C., wax was used with resin to caulk and weather proof ships. Pigmenting the wax resulted in the decoration of warships.

According to a 1st Century historian, encaustic could be used for the painting of portraits on panels, the coloring of marble and terracotta, and for work on ivory. With encaustic the paint could be built-up in relief and the wax gave a rich effect to the pigment. These characteristics made the finished work startlingly life-like.

The nature of encaustic to preserve and color gave it wide use in the stone work of architecture and statuary. Proof of its durability can be found in the Egyptian paintings called the Fayum Portraits, painted in the 2nd Century A.D. as funerary decorations to cover embalmed mummies. They still look fine today.

As an art form, encaustic fell into obscurity in the 9th Century A.D., when it was replaced by fresco, tempera and oil paints.

There is some evidence that encaustic enjoyed a minor revival during the Renaissance period.

Encaustic painting is now growing in popularity – hence the need for an aid to beginners and intermediate artists alike. This booklet aims at saving research time by clarifying the main aspects of encaustic painting and answering questions that you may have as you continue to work in this art form.

I. Setting Up

A - Equipment

B - Tools

C - Wax

D - Containers

E – Supports

A – Equipment

1. Use an Iron (non-steam) or a tack iron to fuse (heat) the first layer onto the support or between layers. An iron will mix the colors differently than a heat gun, i.e., you will have less control over the final color. For bigger areas, use an iron when fusing the first layer onto the wood.

2. Choose a heat gun for more focused fusing. It will also allow you to move the wax more easily.

3. Try a propane/butane/ jeweler's torch for quicker, focused fusing. Some experience is necessary when using a torch, as it works differently than a

heat gun. Careful handling and attention are necessary.

4. Place the painting under a heat lamp until the wax is fluid. This will enable you to work at your leisure as the wax will stay fluid.

5. Place your wax containers on an electrically-heated griddle with a temperature regulator or on an anodized aluminum heated palette.

6. Be sure your griddle or palette is at the right temperature by using a pocket thermometer. Place the thermometer on the griddle to be sure the temperature is correct. Not all temperature regulators work the same. Keep temperature at between 180F – 220F.

7. Use a glass thermometer (available at bakery section of supermarkets) and dip it into the wax container to make sure the wax itself is at the above temperatures and not higher.

B – Tools

1. Use wood 'stamps' to create variety in your design. You will find a number of designs at lumber stores.

2. Experiment with embossing trays.

3. Have a variety of pottery scraping tools. Each one will have a different feel and somewhat different result.

4. Make sure you have a few carving knives to create a variety of grooves and marks.

5. You will find an etching awl useful in the creation of lines.

6. Add a palette knife to your set of tools. It will be useful to scrape wax off of other tools.

7. Brushes:

   a) Use bristle/ natural hair brushes. They are inexpensive and sturdy. Do not use synthetic brushes or brushes with plastic handles as they may burn or melt.

   b) Glaze with sable, badger or ox-hair wash brushes if you want a very smooth surface.

   c) Have greater control of the painting process with brass

filaments heated brushes. (They will require a thermostat and a heat handle. See "Equipment" photo).

d) Clean your brushes with either clear wax paraffin or soy wax. You may also leave them as is, if you dedicate a brush for each color.

e) Alternatively, leave the brushes on a hot griddle. The wax will melt and you will just blot them with paper or cloth.

C – Wax

Wax for encaustics can be lightly, moderately or highly refined.

1. Use yellow nuggets for Lightly Refined wax.

2. Choose white pastilles for Moderately Refined beeswax.

3. Use granules for Highly Refined wax.

4. Mix Microcrystalline with clear wax (one part Microcrystalline to three parts wax) for first layers with more textured surfaces and 3-D effects.

5. Use Encaustic Medium (8%-15% dammar resin plus wax) for ensuing

layers. It produces harder surfaces
and higher sheen.

6. Experiment with plain beeswax
without any additives.

D – Supports

1. Wood

a) Use un-tempered masonite panels
(primed or unprimed). If primed,
you would do best using encaustic
gesso or rabbit skin glue. Acrylic
gesso is not recommended. Sand
the smooth side of the wood to
create a "tooth". Brace the back
to avoid warping if the wood is
not thick enough.

b) Be willing to experiment with
Panel Plywood, birch, hex panel,
Ampersand Claybord or lauan.
The latter will require bracing as it
is thin and tends to warp.

2. Paper

a) Use any thick paper that is
absorbent. Papers can be colored
or hand-made. Mount the paper
on rigid support, as described
under "Wood", ex. masonite, etc.

b) Try Auvergne paper. It's a quality paper from the Auvergne region in France.

c) Experiment with Laminated rag paper or bark paper.

d) Mount heavy watercolor or printmaking paper on rigid backing or support. When working on paper, use beeswax straight without encaustic medium in order to keep the work more pliable. The medium makes the surface harder, which may not work so well with paper. Instead, add microcrystalline to wax 1/3: 2/3, or use the microcrystalline on its own.

e) You may also use unprimed linen or canvas on rigid support (use archival PVA glue to attach the linen or canvas to the support).

E – Containers

1. Use a crock pot to melt the encaustic medium or the clear wax. Crock pots have a "low" and a "high" temperature setting. Either one warms up slowly. Start with the "high" until wax is melted and then keep it at "low".

2. Select electric pans for quicker melting. Keep temperature between 180F and 220F.

3. Use metal cans, muffin tins, metal cupcakes for the individual colors.

4. Cut up soda cans with an X-Acto Knife. Leave a lid for handling (see photo).

5. If you are using an anodized aluminum griddle with bricks or commercial encaustic sticks, melt them directly onto the surface of the griddle.

II. Creating

A - Starting a Painting

1. Cover your ground/support with two or three layers of clear or colored wax. Burn-in (fuse) between layers with an iron, heat gun or torch.

2. Cover the first few layers with beeswax that is mixed with microcrystalline, if you desire increased texture. Otherwise, plain beeswax may be used.

3. Try using medium (medium mixed with beeswax) for the first and last layers. As you keep working, you will discover what works best for you.

4. Use a mixture of medium on its own or mixed with beeswax for harder surfaces. The top layer made with medium will be harder and provide a higher sheen, as well as keep the sheen longer. As you experiment, you will find what works best for you.

B - Glazing

1. Use beeswax mixed with a little color pigment. Remember, glazing is the superimposition of a thin layer of color over another, allowing the color underneath to show while slightly changing its original appearance. For example: if you cover a yellow layer of wax with a thin layer of green, you will still see some of the yellow underneath but the top will be a yellowish green. Glazes affect both the under and the top-layers.

C – Pouring

1. Pour the wax onto the support for thicker shapes. If pouring, you will have less control over the shape, but you can mold it later with the heat gun or the torch.

2. Create a mold into which you will pour the wax, or pour freely. Later, you can heat it into the desired shape or design.

D - Textured Surfaces

1. You may choose to leave the imprint of your brushstrokes after brushing in your color. In that case, fuse the wax lightly so lines and marks remain.

2. Brush one color in one direction, brush another over it in another direction. Burn-in just enough until the top layer of wax shines but is not completely dissolved into the previous layer. You will clearly see the underlying layer. Once you have some experience with the heat gun, you'll have more control of the fusing process.

3. Add collage: paper, beads, plants (dried or not), flowers, straw, found objects, glitter, mica powder, muslin. You may lay paper over one of the layers and add more layers over it. Scrape some of it to let parts of the paper show. These will enrich your work.

4. Etch lines: thin, wide, superficial, deep. Fill in the deeper/wider grooves with a different color of wax or oil paint, fuse it and once it is cold remove the excess, leaving a clean and well defined line or shape.

5. Use stencils. They are very useful and add variety to your design. Stencils made of a thicker material such as plastic are more durable and easier to use and clean. Make sure the stencil is well placed and is flat on your support. If it is not completely flat and adhering to the support, some of the wax will run underneath and the line will not be crisp. Use a blade or a scraper to

clean the excess run-ins, should they occur.

E – Smooth Surfaces

1. Create the appearance of a tile by gently scraping every texture

    off. Burn-in and scrape as many times as needed, until your surface is smooth as glass or marble. A soft brush will create a smoother look.

2. Lightly heat the wood before brushing in the wax, and brush the wax very slowly in one direction. This will give you a very smooth surface.

3. Place the panel on the hot griddle. This will keep the wax fluid and will enable you to work at your leisure.

III – Safety

A – Temperature

1. Keep the temperature of the griddle between 180-220 F. If you see fumes rising from the griddle or palette, quickly decrease the temperature. Fumes are toxic.

2. Be aware that the melting point of beeswax is 143-149 F.

3. Realize that in very cold temperatures, wax will shrink slightly. Layers that have not been well fused together or well fused to the ground or support may separate. Very hot days can soften the wax somewhat but will cause no real damage.

4. Should you use microcrystalline on its own, bear in mind that it melts at 170-180 F. Be aware that the typical melting point of paraffin is 118-165 F.

B – Equipment and Procedures

1. Maintain wax under 220 F. Get a glass wax thermometer for help in determining the correct temperature.

2. Make sure you have good ventilation. It is a plus to have an exhaust fan (preferably near the griddle), and/or a ceiling exhaust, or at least a 3-speed window/door fan. You must have an open door or window. Have good cross ventilation, if possible.

3. Protect your hands with latex gloves.

4. Have potholders around, as well as oven mitts. They will come in handy.

5. Have an all-purpose fire extinguisher. You may never need it but it is safer to have it handy.

6. In cases of higher sensitivity, carbon masks can be useful, although they are somewhat cumbersome.

IV – SUPPLIERS

- Blick Art Materials (a variety of encaustic supplies)
  www.dickblick.com

- The Vermont Country Store (no-steam iron). It is not often found in their catalog but you can get it by contacting them.
  www.vermontcountrystore.com

- United Manufacturers Supply (tacking iron) www.Unitedmfrs.com

- Enkaustikos (a variety of encaustic supplies)
  www.fineartstore.com/enkaustikos

- R&F Handmade Paints (most encaustic supplies)
  www.rfpaints.com

- The Home Depot, Lowe's (heat gun, torches, bristle brushes)

- WalMart, Target (griddle, paraffin)

- Daniel Smith (claybords, brushes, dry pigments, oil paints)
  www.danielsmith.com

- Candlewic (beeswax pastilles, paraffin slabs, microcrystalline)
  www.candlewic.com

- Evans Encaustics
  www.EvansEncaustics.com

- Hobby Stores, supermarkets' baking section (pocket or glass thermometers)

- Encaustic Supplies (paints, waxes, tools, brushes, supports)
  www.encausticsupplies.com

V – Illustrations

A. Containers

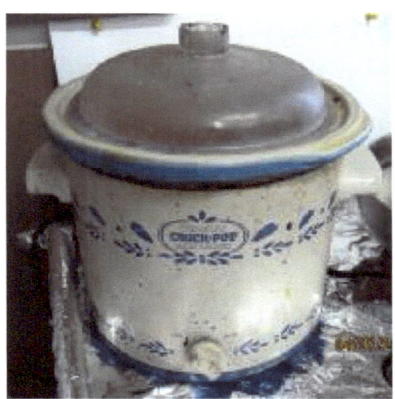

Crock Pot

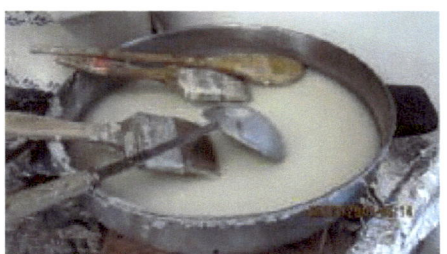

Electric Pan

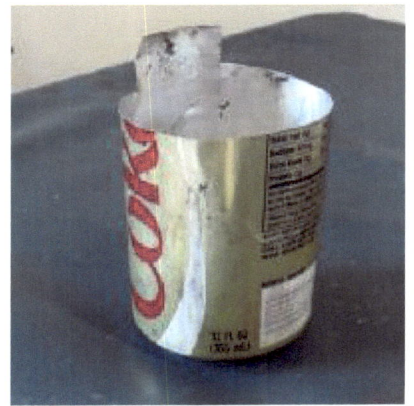

Cut Soda Can

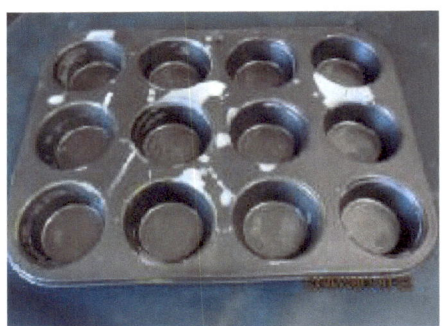

Muffin Tray

B: Equipment

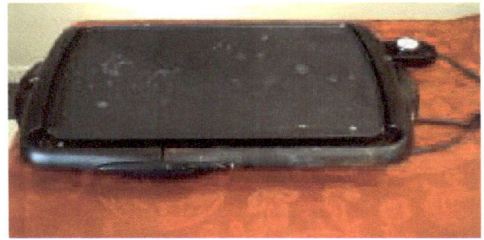

Temperature-controlled Griddle

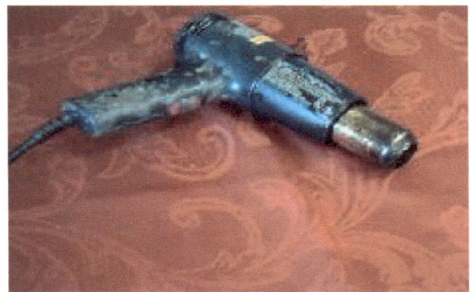

Heat Gun

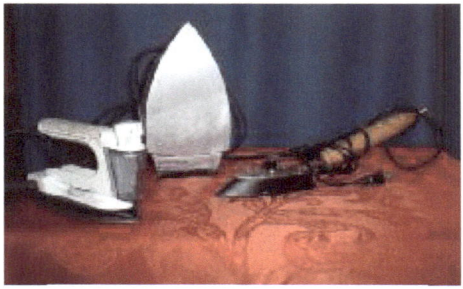

Irons

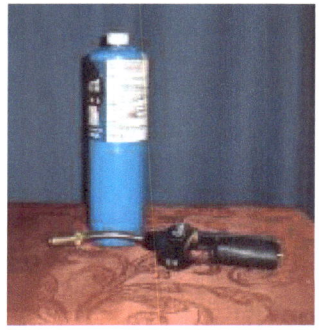

Butane Torch

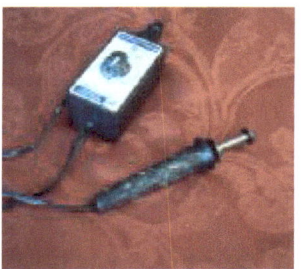

Thermostat and handle

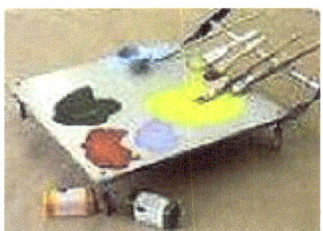

Anodized aluminum palette

C. Miscellaneous

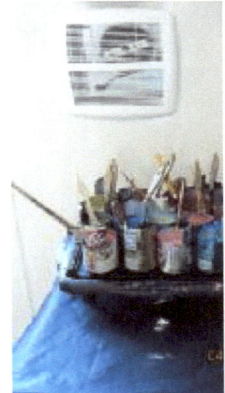

Wall Exhaust by Grill

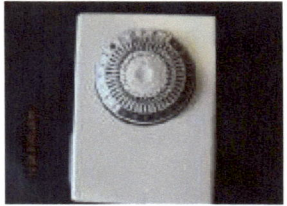

Heavy DutyTimer

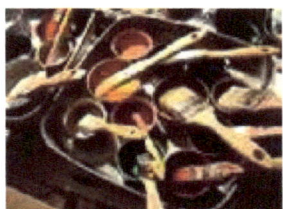

Brushes

ABOUT THE AUTHOR

Bela Fidel was born in Sao Paulo, Brazil, graduated from the Hebrew University in Jerusalem and has lived in the U.S. for over 25 years. She has been painting in oils for over 35 years and has been deeply involved with encaustics since the year 2000.

Her passion for this medium has led her to research its multi-faceted and diverse technical and creative possibilities, which she shares with her students in workshops that she conducts at her Scottsdale studio.

Apart from her passion for art, she is equally, deeply devoted to causes involving animals, both domestic and wild. Her oil series, "Endangered, Threatened and Exploited Species" clearly attest to her love of and concern for all animals.

She lives in Scottsdale, Arizona, with her husband (poet, writer, lyricist, marketing consultant), one dog and two cats.

Contact Information:

Bela Fidel

Bela Fidel Fine Art

http://www.belafidelfineart.com

http://www.belafidel.com

bela@belafidelfineart.com

(480) 221-6947

www.ingramcontent.com/pod-product-compliance
Lightning Source LLC
Chambersburg PA
CBHW041613180526
45159CB00002BC/835